A gift to

_____

from

_____

Published by Changes Forever Publishing House

www.changesforever.com

Text design and layout by Spitfire Design, Upminster

Illustrations by Angie Fairey

Photography Ben Lister *www.benlister.com*

Book cover design by Helen Waller *www.icre8design.co.uk*

Editing completed by Caro Hart *www.franklin-hart.co.uk*

A catalogue record for this book is available from the British Library.

ISBN: 978-0-9572484-0-3

First published in the United Kingdom in 2012 by Changes Forever Publishing House

Who are the flowers
in your garden?

I have asked the two most central flowers in my life to write the foreword to 'Who are the flowers in your garden?'. My parents represent a tree that is solid, reliable, and loving and I realise how lucky I am to have had such a stable family home growing up. It provides the solid base and roots from which I motivate, inspire and support others to be the best they can be in their world.

Foreword

It was a very special and exciting moment when Julie our eldest child was born at the QE II Hospital, Welwyn Garden City in 1966 and our lives changed forever.

It has been so much fun watching her grow up with her sister and two brothers enjoying our house and garden which have provided so many happy memories.

We are so proud that she has matured into a beautiful, intelligent and caring young woman and launched her first book at this very special time in her life.

We hope you will enjoy and benefit from it.

We wish her and Rob every happiness and success in the future.

Terry and Chris Densham

Dedicated to my husband Rob New
and the most special flowers in my life
my daughters Amy and Polly

Introduction by Julie New

The analogy I describe within this little book about the 'garden' is a direct result of my own life experience and has not only helped me to heal following difficult times, but it has also helped countless others just like you.

I became a life coach in 2005 following 20 years in nursing and midwifery. I loved my work, but I just knew I had more to do in the world.

The relationships I have had have taken some unexpected twists and turns and truly taught me the importance of healing and forgiveness.

I soon realised that my passion was to help men and women to thrive, not just survive, following difficult times such as divorce and separation, bereavement and illness. In some cases, it was simply to help them to reach their full potential and live a healthy, happy  and balanced life. It was important to me that I worked with individuals on a personal level rather than through a corporate work environment.

Those clients who sought my help were truly ready to make changes and ready to move forward.

After a couple of years it seemed like the right time to invest in creating a logo and give what I did some kind of identity.

It was then that the Sunflower logo was created. It is a vibrant orange colour, full of life, and it set me thinking.

Life is very much like a garden

We need to put energy into maintaining our everyday lives.

We need to tend the relationships we have with those around us and they will become the flowers in our garden which give us joy.

We need choose carefully the paths we follow in our career and make sure they stay clear and weed free.

It is very easy to allow branches of our lives, such as work, to take priority and ignore the ones that are equally important; we need to achieve balance and harmony in our garden.

We are more than just the gardeners in our own garden, it is the place where we put down roots, from where we take the nourishment we need to grow and develop and to expand into the sunshine. You are the tree at the heart of your garden.

Do you have balance
and harmony
in your garden?

The story of a garden

Once there was a beautiful garden. It had exquisitely manicured lawns of lush green grass. The borders were crammed full of every conceivable plant and variety of flowers.

Each plant was carefully chosen with its position in mind. Their needs were met perfectly in terms of soil type and weather and protection from the elements.

As spring sprang each year the buds would start to develop and eventually colour would magically appear.

The weather provided a balance of rain to hydrate the garden and enough sun to keep everything growing. The sun rose in the morning and set in the evening and the loveliest rainbows appeared when the sun shone and the skies cried with sparkling drops.

At night the stars twinkled in the soft black heavens, sometimes looking like they were caught in the big, safe branches of the trees.

At the central point of the garden was an old but very magnificent oak tree. Its trunk was thick and solid and its roots were deep and healthy.

Other trees grew near-by in an orchard where there were varieties of young saplings of apple, plum and pear.

There were Coxes for munching and
Bramleys for creating hot apple pie and
custard! Amongst the fruit trees were
beehives and the bees buzzed happily
around, each one working away and fulfilling
their life's purpose; to produce the most
delicious honey for miles around.

In another area was a beautiful pond with crystal clear water. The fish were brightly coloured and their magnificent poise and elegance mimicked a ballet. A bench sat quietly by. It was a place of quiet contemplation and reflection.

At the back of the garden was a vegetable plot. Bright rows of carrots, onions and many other more exotic varieties of vegetables flourished. Each growing plant gained energy and vitality from the sunshine and cool rain that fell.

There was a huge blue trampoline in the garden that provided a place of fun and laughter throughout the year for the children, who were now grown and brought their own children to bounce.

The paths were clipped and provided the routes to different parts of the garden. Whichever journey you chose there would be a path to lead you to the right destination.

Birds of all kinds visited the garden and were left food in the winter, when they were at their most hungry.

Blue tits, great tits, a tiny little wren, blackbirds and a beautiful song thrush could be seen, and later they would feed their young. When these were confident and able they were allowed their freedom, to fly away and start life independently.

In the garden lived two guinea pigs; Sniff and Squidge who were very happy, as they were free to roam as they liked.

Sniff was bold and brave with an inquisitive nature and skipped as he walked along. Squidge had a beautiful silky coat, was quite timid and allowed Sniff to lead her through the garden.

The food was abundant and they could sunbathe in the midday sun.
At night they found shelter under the trampoline and could feast on the long juicy grass that couldn't be reached by the large red lawnmower.

The creative director in the garden was an old man by the name of George. He exercised choice over what was grown in the garden and kept tight control over any weeds that strayed into his sanctuary, using an organic method.

HOWEVER

One day, George became very ill. He had a stroke, and so was no longer able to care for his beautiful garden.

The time he had once lavished on nurturing the lush green lawn and flowerbeds was past. His road to recovery was going to be a long one.

Weeds began to appear. At first they weren't particularly visible, but they quickly began to take over.

The energy in the soil sucked into them, leaving the flowers and other plants struggling to survive.

They were hardly able to breathe and their memory and ability to grow almost gone. Snails and slugs began to multiply and slowly tracked across the garden, leaving trails of shiny destruction behind them.

The rain became a storm and the strong winds lashed against the saplings. Struggling against the gale, their shallow roots tore from the ground, leaving them weak and unable to survive.

The storm gained in strength, tearing through the air and across the once beautiful garden. Devastation ensued and finally it grew quiet.

27

Sniff and Squidge came out from the safety of the trampoline. The long grass had protected them and they had survived the strong winds that had reached most areas of the garden. They looked to the sun and stretched out their silky bodies. Looking up they saw the familiar, solid oak tree. A few branches broken, but the main part of the tree remained intact. Its roots were still solid in the ground.

Even more deeply rooted than his mighty oak, George fought back to health. One day, he was well enough to enter his garden again and his energy began to return. He had realised that he needed help, not only with his life, but with his precious garden. He began to realise how important the people in his life were to him.

His family and special friends started clearing parts of the garden. This enabled him to spend time on the bench contemplating, thinking and reflecting. It meant he once again had contact with the people he truly loved and cared for.

The guinea pigs enjoyed his company and the birds returned to nest in the bushes and in the solid arms of the oak.
The vegetable plot became more productive and new vibrant flowers appeared and the weeds were once more kept at bay.

A balance was created, and George was able to enjoy the beauty of the garden once more, as well as working within and it was a good place to be. The experience had taught him many lessons.

In the past he had taken life for granted; his grand-children had grown up without him realising. The enjoyment he gained from sharing his special place with his beloved wife, his friends and family now outshone the memories of the past.

He could see a future and was able to move on. The past remained in another part of the garden. It was still there, but no longer as painful. It had become a memory, and as a memory was welcome now to stay for ever.

You are probably wondering what happened to Sniff and Squidge. Well, they lived for many years and their babies continued to live happily in the long lush grass under the trampoline!

After many long happy guinea-pig years, when they died, as is natural in a garden, they were buried at the back of the border and everyone remembered them when they saw the flowers waving in the breeze.

What is this flower and garden thing all about?

Life on earth can be both an interesting and challenging experience. We are all presented with situations and sometimes as human beings we forget we have choice to lead our lives in any way we see fit. We can choose how we feel at any given moment and that is something we lose sight of when our garden becomes over grown and chaotic.

I guess that is where the saying "I can't see the wood for the trees" comes from.

It is why we lose sight of the importance of balance in our lives. If our garden is clear and well defined, our minds are clear. If the grass needs cutting and the weeds are allowed to take over, it becomes less likely that we can clearly see the path that is in front of us.

We can learn how to achieve balance and harmony from the inspiring stories of others and I am going to tell you some of those stories.

The garden helps me every day to cope and to see the beauty and wonder of what is happening all around me.

The metaphor of the garden can be used to illustrate everything we experience as a human being; even coping with life and death situations.

Rob

I think I should start with the true love of my life, Rob. (I am actually writing this in Italy in the warm sunshine. The breeze is warm and the birds are singing, cherry blossom is on the trees and the grass is rustling. It seems appropriate to be writing about a relationship that has deep, strong roots that will withstand the storms and occasional hurricanes that hit from time to time.)

In 1992, Rob was a fit healthy vital man with his life stretching before him. He relished life and he worked hard and played each and every day.

Rob had met his future wife and they were six weeks away from getting married and were planning a family. His passion was for motocross and this particular weekend was special. His fiancée had bought him a brand new bike and she was coming to watch him race for the first time. He was keen to win.

Nearing the end of the race he came off his bike mid-air and the bike followed, crushing his body. Rob knew immediately that he was paralysed. The paramedic team took him to Stoke Mandeville Hospital and that began the slow journey of healing and the process of grieving for the active life he had before.

Rob spent a year in Stoke Mandeville Hospital and when he returned home their relationship which he thought was so strong came to an abrupt end.

He returned to work, only to be given the task of relocating the factory to another country and finally being made redundant, along with the entire workforce.

He recently reflected on that time in relation to the garden analogy and realised that the trunk of his tree had been damaged, as if his tree had been struck by lightning.
The healing process has taken many years.
Physical pain passes, emotional pain can take a lot longer.

My dear friend Jeanie

Jeanie talked to me about when she had breast cancer. The disease appeared from nowhere. She was 42, enjoying her life, gaining strength from doing something she loved as a holistic practitioner; she was caring for others, healing them and helping them gain in strength and positive energy.

However, her own area of the garden was becoming less well tended. The busier she got the less she thought about herself.
If you use the analogy of Jeanie being the tree her very roots were beginning to dry out and only certain branches were flourishing.

Where was the balance in Jeanie's garden?

The person Jeanie was neglecting was herself as she was in fact prioritising her work too much.

Jeanie's family have always been of paramount importance in her life and yet the close relationship she once shared with her only sister had become a little strained over a storm that had hit.

The interesting thing was that during the battle with cancer, she was surrounded by a strong array of 'flowers'. They came from all over the world either virtually or to her home. The experience made her realise how abundant her personal garden was.

It was full of incredible positivity and even in her darkest hour, she felt the love of her nearest and dearest, her true flowers.

The relationship with her sister was effectively being watered and fed again as they saw more of each other. Jeanie felt and saw the deep love and affection her sister had for her. She made homemade soup, visited regularly, and provided practical help and their relationship started to heal and come back to life.

I guess sometimes we have to accept that all flowers are different. They have different qualities and their true colours are sometimes difficult to see until a storm has passed. A little like the story of George's garden.

Is there balance
in your garden?

The Garden Effect

The garden effect began almost as soon as the sunflower design was created.
The thought struck me that the relationships we form and the lives we lead resemble a garden in all its many forms, shapes, sizes and colours.

It has enabled people to view their own situation from different perspectives. I have personally watched it take effect and work its magic.

Beverley and Julie

Beverley is my sister. We were born seven years apart and I don't have a clear memory of her as I was growing up. We became close when she had a serious accident in her early 20s. She was in Australia when it happened and when she came home, our relationship blossomed. She became a true flower in my garden. We laughed and cried together and supported one another.

She was the one who realised I was a flower wilting fast and needed a bit of care and attention.

At home I was working hard as a midwife, organising the house, caring for my girls who were small, running a home-based business and coping with my husband's demanding work schedule as a police officer.

My garden was out of balance, I had no time to nurture myself, the central tree.

I was thrilled when she gave me a ticket to the sunshine where she was running Pilates retreat breaks. That week, doing the things that make me sparkle, nourished and tended me and brought me back to life.

The garden effect is available for everyone to learn from and make sure relationships are as rich as they can be Many people now refer to their friends as "flowers" and also recognise when the balance is uneven, through relating their experience to the garden analogy.

Life isn't a bed of roses, but you are the gardener in your own garden of life.

You have the power to make the changes and choose who is welcome at any given time.

Cherry

Cherry swam into the world and gazed at her mother with wide eyes through her perspex crib in the hospital. She, her mother and father connected on a very deep level. From that moment she felt the love of her parents.

She was safe in the knowledge that she had firm roots like a solid oak tree.

That tree was shaken with the divorce of her parents but this was nothing in comparison to her experience when the main roots were torn from the ground when her father died very suddenly.

When Cherry was told she sat numb and unable to feel and went from being a happy flower, to a very angry unhappy teenager.

She started harming herself and making herself sick and no longer surrounded herself with her true flowers.

Over time, with the help of her mother and those who loved her, she began to relax, heal and that wide eyed baby seedling returned.

Now she has finally began developing her own roots and finding out what she needs to make the flower within flourish and grow.

I can clearly see how children can grow into their adult lives very disturbed if they are not allowed to feel their pain and eventually reach acceptance. My life's work is to ensure children are able to enter their adult lives healthy healed and happy. Like work in a garden this takes time work and sustained effort, to ensure that all important balance is achieved.

Bereavement is a process we have to go through and blocking it can create challenges later in life.

The garden can be used to think about everything we experience as a human being; even losing a loved one.

Helen

I worked as a coach with Helen who asked me why she lost her husband at a very young age. I said there was not an easy answer to her question. For 20 years she had felt the grief and got very stuck in the painful part.

We reflected on the situation using the analogy of the garden and she said she suddenly felt better because she realised that although her husband was no longer with her physically he hadn't actually left her completely. Effectively he had just gone to another part of her garden where he would live on forever.

Thinking about her situation in a different way, allowed her to move on. She admitted to me that it might be quite nice to meet someone who she could share her life.

Her family were wonderful but they all had their own gardens to tend and care for. She realised that her beloved husband would always be there and that would never change, but she could now tackle her life with renewed energy and passion.

Once you get the idea of the garden, it can have a startling effect on how you think; you start using it, almost unconsciously, to take a fresh look at your world.

Caro and Elizabeth

My friend Caro is proud of the way in which her daughter Elizabeth has left home for University; she is doing well at her studies, has made good friends and is happy and busy. Caro raised Elizabeth single-handedly from the time she was four years old, while holding down a full time job and for several years, studying part-time for a masters' degree.

Recently, Caro's life changed, she was made redundant and found she was suffering from health problems. She began to re-evaluate her life and realised that she hadn't been much of a "muddy-puddle" sort of a mum.

Caro and I had met by this time and she
knew about the garden and wondered
if she had taken the best care she could
of her own special flower.

Then on Mothers' Day a home-made card
arrived and Caro was immediately struck by
the lush flowers pasted around the front.
Inside the card, Elizabeth had chosen pictures
of them at special moments in their lives;
picking flowers in the countryside;
the day trip to Versailles when Caro
graduated, the night before Elizabeth went
to South Africa for a month on a World
Challenge, the morning Elizabeth's A level
results came through and they knew she had
her place at University.

At the end of the card, Elizabeth had written;
"Thank you for being there with me, giving me support when I needed you and stepping back when I needed to stand by myself.
I couldn't have asked for any more."
Caro realised that their roots together were true and strong.

Her daughter had grown into a strong and beautiful tree, giving back in abundance the care and support she had received.

They may each now be working in their own gardens, but the connections will always remain.

Are you ready
to branch out?

I have spoken of how storms and challenges, even death, can be understood using the garden. In some ways, we already have the analogy there; we speak of big changes in our lives as being "uprooted", we talk of "branching out" when we are trying something new. We just need to trust that the garden will help us to cope in difficult stormy situations.

Alice and Sol

This is a story of strength, love, joy and passion. In 1986 two young people met outside the Hippodrome in London and there was an instant connection.

A seed was planted in the ground and, despite the distance between these two people; one living in Holland and the other an Italian in England, the roots started to develop over a period of five years when they wrote to one-another and visited each other's homes.

The relationship flourished, grew and eventually Sol agreed to settle in Holland.

Alice was reluctant to leave her homeland as it would mean leaving her mother. She was raised by this strong woman in a wonderfully nurturing 'can do' culture. She was given freedom and trust. She was a sensitive, quiet peace-loving child whose greatest love was, and still is, family. Nothing was the same for Alice from the age of nine years old when the knock at the door revealed that her father had been killed in an horrific accident. At that moment she was uprooted and felt unable to come to terms with her loss.

The process of settling in a new country was not easy for Sol. The language created barriers to growth at work and the relationship between him and Alice's mother became strained. Alice realised that for the security, health and wellbeing of her own family, they had to go. Twelve years on Alice still feels the pain of when she was uprooted again, this time from her homeland and the family she was born into. She knows, however, that the roots she has developed with her husband in England are strong and healthy and they have created a loving family. They have four beautiful children and their home is often filled with the sound of laughter. In their garden is planted a tree for each family member.

After a challenge or crisis, after a storm has ravaged our garden in other words, we need the help of family and friends, as George did. Although we have to do the growing, they can water and fertilize, nurture and sustain us. Were you wondering what happened next to Rob? Well…

Rob and Julie

Rob's redundancy set him on a new path and he became a very talented design engineer and worked from home knowing that one day the right woman would appear.

That woman was me!

Our friendship grew as we spent time together laughing and understanding one another. From early on the roots were growing deep into the ground. We nurtured our relationship with time and effort.
My two girls Amy and Polly loved Rob and could see how happy I was with him and it seemed more sensible for us to move in with him.

Poor Rob was invaded as we also brought our Ollie,our black Labrador, two guinea pigs and Tinkerbelle the hamster!

It took time to adjust to the change and over the years various challenges have struck our lives. I talk about storms and hurricanes affecting our gardens and the tragic death of the girls' beloved father Richard was more like a tornado. It hit without warning and caused more damage than you would ever imagine.

The garden effect came into effect once more. Our roots together were deep and healthy and although the surface branches were damaged the core of our relationship and that of our family unit remained strong.

Having the knowledge of the "garden" helped us to work at healing and become strong once more.

Rob's health continued to fluctuate greatly and when one challenge was over the waters would be calm and still before the next torrent. Ill health has struck many times since I have been with Rob.

Recently he developed a very acute infection that saw him in hospital for 10 weeks. Unfortunately I received a call early one morning to say they wanted me to come in urgently as he wasn't expected to survive. When I arrived, I was told to expect the worst which made me think of my garden; it helped.

The Lister Hospital team worked tirelessly and by the end of the day his condition was stable.

Some days later, we spent time thinking about our life together, holding hands and connecting with our eyes. He asked me: "Will you marry me?" My heart skipped a beat and I replied without hesitation "Yes!"

Like a garden the analogy continues to grow and develop. It would be impossible to take the path away from the challenges we face.

I choose to see the wealth and abundance and richness he brings to my life and has enabled us to stay together on the path with him hand in hand.

On reflection the branches of both our individual trees over the years had begun to regenerate. Rob's branches were growing in different directions to those he had relied upon before and his roots were being nourished in a warm lively home, surrounded by people, and pets, who loved him.

Our marriage ceremony on New Year's Eve 2011 brought together our entire garden.

It was full of flowers, herbs, shrubs and trees. The candlelit blessing represented us coming together as a family and the whole day was centred on the roots of a tree including the the cake which had a tree on top with us resting under it together.

Whatever the future holds for us Rob will always be in my garden and he in mine.

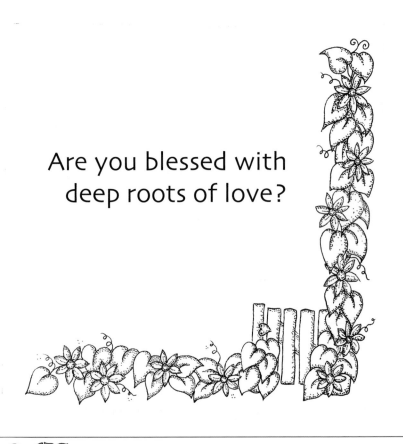

Are you blessed with
deep roots of love?

Who are the flowers in YOUR garden?

Life is what you make it. If we take a step back and look at our own garden we can make sure it is the best it can be. You can start putting that in practice right now:

*Challenge one: **Your own garden***

Make some notes and think about your own garden. Start to think about the ways in which you nurture your flowers and are nurtured in turn. Think about the paths you take and the different areas in your garden. Ask yourself these questions, you may also come up with others.

How does your own garden feel? What does it look like? What sounds do you hear?

Is it heart-centred?

Where are you now and where do you want to be?

Do you nurture yourself and take time for you?

Notes

Challenge two: **Who are the flowers?**

I want you to take a step back and have a little think about these questions.

 Who are the flowers?

 Are there any weeds?

Get a piece of paper and draw up two columns.

 Flowers:

An example of a flower may be something or someone that makes you feel good

 Weeds:

An example of a weed maybe unwanted clutter, a relationship that isn't going well. You will know what are representing weeds in your life. Remember these exercises are for your eyes only

Go ahead…..

MY GARDEN

FLOWERS   WEEDS

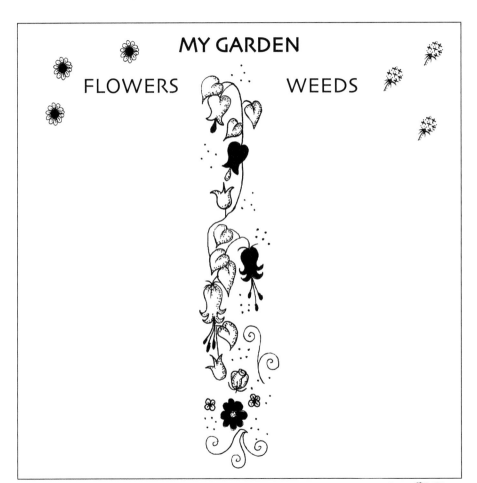

Notes

Challenge three: **How is your central tree growing? Is the tree stable with deep healthy roots?**

It is crucial that we develop good relationships first and foremost with ourselves. I hear so often that people don't put themselves first and the impact can be devastating long term. It helps you to work out what is truly important and to recognise what is important to maintain a healthy balance.

This is incredibly important. I want you to imagine you are the central tree in your life.

Think first about the roots of your tree. Are they deep, strong and healthy? What values do you hold and where did they come from? What do you believe? To flourish the tree has needs and so what does it need?

Here is the trunk of a tree for you to work on.

Next draw the branches of your tree; what are the different branches of your life? They may not immediately be apparent, but they are just waiting to start sprouting. Give time to allow your thoughts to come and start drawing…

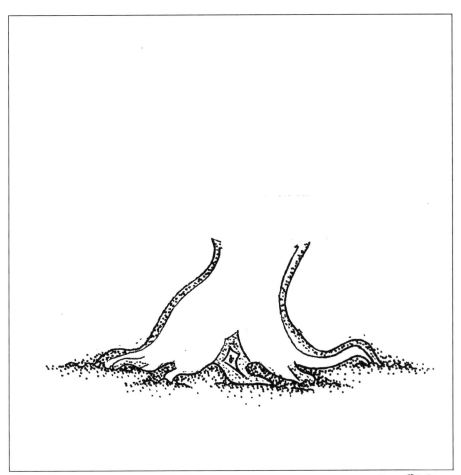

79

Think about how the different branches of your tree are growing. Are there any which are developing more slowly than the others? A tree needs to be in balance, so what do you need to do about these branches? Think about the branches you have drawn on your tree and maybe some of these other branches:

 Career

 Money

 Health

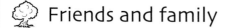 Friends and family

Significant other/ romance

 Personal growth

 Fun and recreation

 Physical environment

 Spirituality

I suggest you take a look at your tree every six months or so to check in on where you are...

Notes

Challenge four: **Taking time for yourself**

FINALLY, ASK YOURSELF:

> What difference would it make to you
> and those people around you if you did
> spend time on you?

NEVER FORGET

YOU are important in your own garden and
the better care you take of the life you create
on this earth, the more it will be the best it
can possibly be…

Notes

Conclusion

I hope you have gained an understanding of the powerful garden metaphor that I have grown over the past few years.

It has been very relevant to many of my clients, friends family and colleagues and I regularly receive emails and comments about how much different parts of the garden analogy have helped in the understanding of a relationship or restoring the balance and health in a relationship that hasn't been nurtured.

I hope you can take something from this short book that reflects how important it is to remember to nurture relationships.

I hope that the stories I have told you inspire and motivate you. I hope you have also seen how important it is to look after yourself and to allow the flowers in your garden to help you to grow as you have done for them

Nurture your flowers. Keep the weeds under control and never forget to keep deepening your roots and working to be a balanced and healthy tree.

Enjoy growing and flourishing personally and professionally.

Warmest wishes

Julie New
Founder and Inspiration Changes Forever

I endeavour to nurture
myself everyday in all weathers.
Do you?

Are you ready to
make any changes
to your life?

About the author

Julie New was a senior nurse and midwife until 2005 when she left the NHS and started training to become a life coach. She had been coached herself since 1999 and had made significant change as a result.

She became founder and inspiration behind the organisation Changes Forever following the development of her analogy where she likens 'relationships and life' as being like a garden.
Changes Forever in time will become known as a special place that will enable, inspire and support people like YOU to be the best you can possibly be in your world.

At the launch of the Changes Forever website a new member said: "I was wondering who this woman was that my cousin had told me so much about. When I heard her speak, I was puzzled; she doesn't come over like an evangelist, and yet I could simply see how much impact her message had on the people there and so many in the future.

"When I met her and sat down with her, I began to understand. She is passionate about personal growth, her ideas about the garden and her plans for Changes Forever, bubble out and you feel yourself wanting to help make that happen. She is completely sincere and genuinely wants to reach as many people as possible to help them to make the changes they need in their lives.

"But, above all, Julie exudes what psychologists call unconditional positive regard. She is genuinely interested in the people she meets, she values them, no matter who they are and she is driven to make things better for them. You never know quite where you are going to land up being with Julie, but you know it will be a great experience!"

When Julie works with you, she uses her intuition and what she gives you is a chest full of treasure; invaluable and priceless. As a life and business coach, she asks probing, sometimes difficult and life-changing questions. She is kind, loving, effervescent and fun to be with and uses her own life experiences (which have been challenging) to help you **change your life forever**.